C000212736

FOR USE IN U.S.A ONLY

ISBN 0-933546-39-4

9 780933 546394

KHANIQAHI-NIMATULLAHI
(NIMATULLAHI SUFI ORDER)

306 West 11th Street
New York, New York 10014
Tel: 212-924-7739

4021 19th Avenue
San Francisco,
California 94132
Tel: 415-586-1313

4931 MacArthur Blvd. NW
Washington, D.C. 20007
Tel: 202-338-4757

84 Pembroke Street
Boston,
Massachusetts 02118
Tel: 617-536-0076

310 NE 57th Street
Seattle, Washington 98105
Tel: 206-527-5018

11019 Arleta Avenue
Mission Hills, Los Angeles,
California 91345
Tel: 818-365-2226

4642 North Hermitage
Chicago, Illinois 60640
Tel: 312-561-1616

405 Greg Avenue
Santa Fe, New Mexico 87501
Tel: 505-983-8500

219 Chace Street
Santa Cruz, California 95060
Tel: 408-425-8454

95 Old Lansdowne Road
West Didsbury, Manchester M20
8NZ, England
Tel: 061-434-8857

Kölner Strasse 176
5000 Köln 90
West Germany
49-2203-15390

Van Blankenburgstraat 66B
2517 XS The Hague
Netherlands
070-450251

41 Chepstow Place
London W2 4TS,
England
Tel: 01-229-0769

DOGS

FROM THE SUFI POINT OF VIEW

Also available by Dr. Javad Nurbakhsh

1. In the Tavern of Ruin: Seven Essays on Sufism
2. In the Paradise of the Sufis
3. What the Sufis Say
4. Masters of the Path
5. Divani Nurbakhsh: Sufi Poetry
6. Sufism (I): Meaning, Knowledge and Unity
7. Traditions of the Prophet, Vol.1
8. Sufism (II): Fear and Hope, Contraction and Expansion,Gathering and Dispersion, Intoxication and Sobriety, Annihilation and Subsistence
9. The Truths of Love: Sufi Poetry
10. Sufi Women
11. Traditions of the Prophet, Vol. II
12. Jesus in the Eyes of the Sufis
13. Spiritual Poverty in Sufism
14. Sufism III
15. Sufi Symbolism I
16. The Great Satan, "Eblis'
17. Sufi Symbolism II
18. Sufism IV
19. Sufi Symbolism III

DOGS

From the Sufi Point of View

By
Dr. Javad Nurbakhsh

KHANIQAHI-NIMATULLAHI PUBLICATIONS
LONDON NEW YORK

Translated under the supervision of Dr. Javad Nurbakhsh
by Terry Graham, with the collaboration of Neil and Sima
Johnston and Ali-Reza Nurbakhsh
Designed by Jane Lewisohn

Distributed by:
Kegan Paul International Ltd., P.O. Box 256
118 Bedford Court Mansions
Bedford Avenue
London WC 1B 3SW
ISBN 0-7103-0364-5

British Library Cataloguing in Publication Data
Dogs from a Sufi Point of View
1. Sufi tales and Legends
I. Nurbakhsh, Javad, 1927
II. [*Sag as didga-e Sufiyan;* English]
398.2' 0956
ISBN 0-935546-39-4

Published by Khaniqahi-Nimatullahi Publications
41 Chepstow Place
London W2 4TS
England
Telephone: 01-229-0769

Printed by Morning Litho Printers Ltd. in Great Britain (TU)
Tel: 01-474-3801

CONTENTS

ILUSTRATIONS

COVER

Composite drawing of a dog made up of birds, done in the provincial Mughal style approximately 18th century. B.M. London.

INTRODUCTION

Before embarking on discussion of the Sufis' attitude towards the dog and commenting on the dogs attributes, let me first introduce this text by quoting 'Ali ebn Abi Ṭāleb, the seminal figure of Sufism:

Happy is the one who leads the life of a dog! For the dog has ten characteristics which every believer should possess. First, the dog has no status among creatures; second, the dog is a pauper having no worldly goods; third, the entire earth is his resting place; fourth, the dog goes hungry most of the time; fifth, the dog will not leave his master's door even after having received a hundred lashes; sixth, he protects his master and his friend, and when someone approaches he will attack the foe and let the friend pass; seventh, he guards his master by night, never sleeping; eighth, he performs most of his duties silently; ninth, he is content with whatever his master gives him; and tenth, when he dies, he leaves no inheritance. (RJn I 414)

Elsewhere 'Ali has said, "Amongst dogs, good is found only in the hunting and sheep dogs."

Two conclusions may be drawn from this second quotation. The first is that in Islam and Sufism, knowledge and training are so important that even a trained dog is considered a respected model, being of some value as opposed to an untrained dog which is regarded as having no value. The second is that the Sufi master, when instructing people, utilizes this same idea to teach them that in addition to benefiting from the society in which they live, they must also serve and contribute to the well-being of that society. The idle individual is like a stray dog, worthless and unproductive, while the useful individual, like the dog that is beneficial to society, is valuable to that society and worthy of respect.

PART ONE

SUFI MASTERS AND DOGS

PREFACE

In the Middle East, the dog has traditionally been regarded as a foul and ritually impure being, the most despicable of creatures, to be driven away by most people. Not only would the dog not be fed, but it would often be beaten or stoned.

Only hunting dogs and sheep dogs were looked upon with favor by a few people, and then only as slaves or beasts of burden, like the donkey, which was treated with contempt. Such dogs were rare compared to the many packs of stray dogs.

Given the nature of the dog's treatment by society, it is not surprising that dogs would tend to respond to the abuse and starvation afflicted upon them in a ferocious and savage manner. Most stray dogs lived on the outskirts of towns, in and on the rooftops of derelict buildings. They shunned mankind by day, coming out only at night to roam the streets, searching for the most meagre sustenance from the scraps and bones thrown away by the people of the villages and towns.

In the literature of this region, the dog is the symbol of foulness and ferocity, savagery and viciousness, and in everyday language, the word 'dog' was used as the vilest of insults.

The first group of people to react against society's injustice towards the dog were the Sufis, who strove to show people that the dog possessed virtuous qualities, qualities which many human beings, regarding themselves as the noblest of God's creatures, lacked.

Sufis made a point of holding the poverty and wretchedness of the dog in special esteem, considering themselves to be the dogs, or less than the dogs, of the lane of the Beloved.

To direct people's attention to the positive qualities of the dog, they sometimes cited the dog in Lailā's lane, which was stroked and treated with respect by Majnun. Their view was that the whole world is God's lane, that the dog is God's creation like everything else, and that even the dog has a place in God's lane. Anyone who loves God must love the dog of His lane as well.

On occasion Sufis refered to their own *nafs* [1] as a 'dog', saying, " If you are a human being, rid yourself of the base dog-like *nafs!* Be its foe! It takes no skill to abuse the outward dog, but bringing the inward dog to heel is the work of men!"

In this work we have sought to represent the view of the dog as presented in Sufi writings.

[1] Unless otherwise indicated, the term *nafs* used in this volume refers to ego, selfish desires, and desires of the ego.

The following passages illustrate the kinds of encounters that the great Sufis had with dogs. These stories are drawn from classical Sufi literature.

It is said that Bāyazid was out walking with his companions one day when he happened upon a dog in a narrow passageway coming the other way. Bāyazid backtracked to a point where the dog could pass and then beckoned him forward. At this, one of his disciples had the following negative thought: "God has elevated man above all else. How is it that Bāyazid, the monarch of all gnostics, with his rank and all these sincere disciples, has given preference to a dog?" In response, Bāyazid said, "Dear friends, the dog addressed me in the language of state, saying, 'Bāyazid, what did I do wrong in pre-eternity and you do right, that I should be dressed in the skin of a dog and you in the robes of the monarch of gnostics?' This question came into my inner consciousness, so I gave way to him." (TA 172)

It is related that Bāyazid was out walking one day when a dog fell in beside him. The master pulled the hem of his robe away from the dog. The dog exclaimed, "If I am dry and touch you, there is no difficulty between us, and if I am wet and touch you, the ritual purification[1] will cleanse you. But if you wrap your cloak around your 'self' (*nafs*), not even ablution in the seven seas will make you pure."

Bāyazid replied to the dog, "You are outwardly impure and I inwardly. Come let us put the two together so that the combination will bring purity to both of us." The dog then said, "You are not worthy of my companionship, for I am rejected by mankind while you are accepted. Stones are thrown at me while you are greeted as the 'Monarch of the Gnostics'. I never leave so much as a bone for tomorrow but you have a whole crock of wheat stored up." Bāyazid replied, "If I am not a worthy companion to a dog, how can I accompany the Eternal? Glory be to God Who cultivates the finest of creation through the basest thereof!" (TA 172; MN 314)

[1] According to Islamic custom if a wet dog touches one's clothes, the clothes should be ritually washed seven times in water or dust.

It is told that Noah, encountering a dog one day, exclaimed, "How ugly this dog is! How unpleasant is its face!" God's reproach immediately flashed upon him, "O Noah, do you criticize Our creation? Are you better than him?" Noah wept at the lesson in this rebuke. He wept so long and piteously that he was named 'Lamentation', *(nauḥ*, the Arabic for Noah). (KAM IV 381)

Dho'n-Nun Meṣri was seen one day sitting and eating some bread with a dog. For every bite he took for himself, he threw a morsel to the dog. The people asked, "Why don't you marry and have children, so that you can feed *them?*" Dho'n-Nun replied, "If I feed the dog, he keeps watch over me when I sleep. This is better than feeding a wife and children who would keep me from God!" (MRM 412)

It is said Jonaid was out walking with a disciple one night when a dog suddenly barked. Jonaid exclaimed, "At your service! At your service!" When the disciple asked him what state this was, Jonaid replied, "I perceived the power of the dog's bark to be God's wrath and a reflection of divine power, but I was unaware of the dog itself, so I answered 'At your service!' " (TA 427)

Shebli said, "I learned Sufism from a dog who was sleeping by the door of a house. The master of the house came out and drove it away, but the dog came back. I said to myself, 'How wretched this dog is! When driven away, he still comes back.' The dog, commanded by God, said, 'O Shaikh, where should I go? He is my master.' " (KAM I 447)

When Ḥasan Baṣri saw a dog one day, he exclaimed, "O Lord, accept me as a dog, like this one!" Someone asked him, "Which is the better, you or the dog?" Ḥasan replied, "If I am spared God's torment, then I am the better; if not, by God's might, he is better than a hundred like me!" (TA 41)

It is recounted that Ma'ruf Karkhi had an uncle who was the governor of his township. One day, passing by a derelict site, the uncle noticed Ma'ruf sitting, eating and sharing his meal with a dog. For every morsel Ma'ruf put in his own mouth, he put another in that of the dog. His uncle asked, "Have you no shame, eating with a dog?" Ma'ruf replied, "It is my own shame before the dog that makes me give him food." (TA 326)

It is related that Abu 'Abdo'llāh Torughbodi was dining with his disciples one day when Ḥallāj had, just returned from Kashmir. Ḥallāj was wearing a black robe and leading two black dogs. Torughbodi told his disciples of Ḥallāj's approach, saying to them, "Go and welcome him, for Ḥallāj is an important man." The disciples did as Torughbodi said, meeting Ḥallāj who arrived leading the two dogs. Ḥallāj made straight for the master, who rose and gave Ḥallāj his place. Ḥallāj sat down with his dogs at the meal. When the disciples saw their master receiving Ḥallāj warmly, yielding his place to Ḥallāj, they said nothing but were inwardly disturbed. The master saw to it that Hallāj ate and fed the dogs. When Ḥallāj had eaten, he rose to leave and Torughbodi saw him off. Upon the Master's return, the disciples asked him, 'O master, what is happening that you let a dog sit in your place and send us to welcome such a person, throwing the entire company into ritual impurity?" The master replied, "Indeed Ḥallāj's dog is a servant. It runs after him and remains beside him, while our dog lies within us; and we run after it. There is a world of difference between thoes who follow their dog and those whose dog follows them. Ḥallāj's dog can be seen outwardly, while yours remains hidden within you. That is a thousand times worse." Their master concluded by saying, "Ḥallāj will be the king of creation, whether he has a dog or not. He will be granted success." (TA 556)

Abu 'Othmān Ḥiri said, "For forty years I have not been discontented with any situation which God has put me in." The following is an example of what he meant:

A adversary of Abu 'Othmān once invited him to his home. When Abu 'Othmān arrived at the man's door, he was told, "Go home you glutton of a shaikh; there's nothing here!" At this, Abu 'Othmān turned away. Abu 'Othmān had taken only a few steps when the man called him again, saying, "O shaikh, come back!" He turned back and the man said, "You are quite persistent when it comes to getting a bite to eat! Go away! There is even less than before!" Again Abu 'Othmān turned away and again he was called back. This time he was told that there was nothing but stone to eat and that if he did not want it, he should leave once again. So, again he left.

This happened thirty times, being invited, then driven away, and yet there appeared no change within him. Finally the man broke down, threw himself at Abu 'Othmān's feet, wept, repented, and became his disciple, saying, "What a man you are! Thirty times you were humiliated and driven off and yet you remain unaffected!"

Abu 'Othmān explained, "This is not difficult. It is the

طاسی دلخته راهر شام مسوزی چوشمع
ایستی راخوش غشی چرب بدا کردۀ

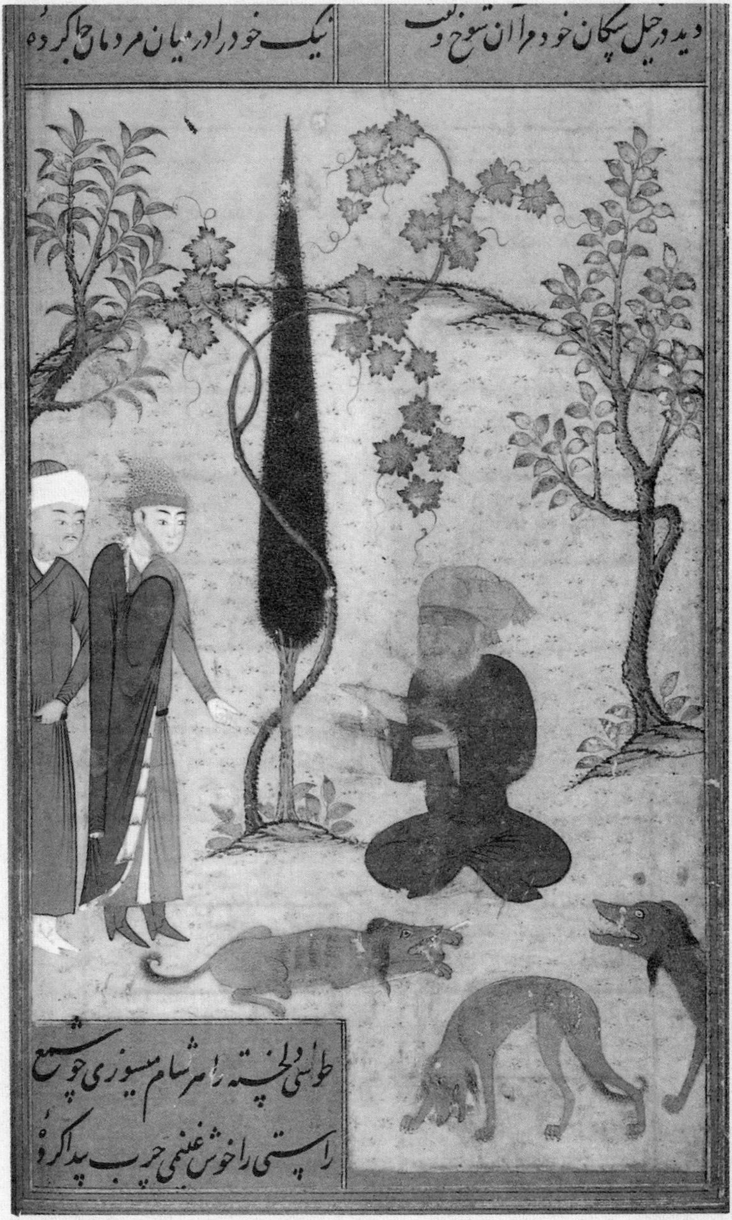

Plate 1:

Two young men come upon an old man sitting among a pack of scavenging dogs. The couplet at the top of the picture describes the interaction between one young man and the old man;

Seeing me seated among a pack of dogs
That flippent sweetheart sneered and said:
"How fine at last you have managed
To find yourself a place among men!"

This is an illustration for a ghazal by Abdullah Tusi who was a native of Khorasan (d. 1490). It is found in an anthology produced in Shirvan (Shmakha), done in the northern provincial Timurid style and dated 1468. (Add. 16561, f. 85b., B.L., London.)

way of dogs. When you drive them away, they go, and when you call them back, they come. No change can be detected in them. This is of no consequence; dogs are equal to us in performing it. The work of men is something else." (TA 478)

It is reported that Abo'l-Qāsem Naṣrābādi performed the pilgrimage forty times with trust-in-God (*tawakkol).* One day he saw a dog in Mecca, hungry, thirsty and wasted. Having nothing to give it, he asked if there was anyone who would buy the merit of his forty Pilgrimages with a loaf of bread. Someone accepted the offer, which was duly witnessed, and the master gave the bread to the dog. An advanced visionary saw this and emerged from a corner to reproach Abo'l-Qāsem, saying, "You fool! Did you think you were doing something, selling off forty Pilgrimages for a loaf of bread when my master [Adam] sold heaven for two grains of wheat? There are over a thousand grains in this loaf!" When the master heard this, he retreated to a corner and dropped his head in shame. (TA 778)

Abu Sho'aib Moqanna', known for his righteousness, was a resident of Egypt and a contemporary of Abu Sa'id Kharrāz. He had undertaken seventy Pilgrimages on foot, beginning each journey by donning the *eḥrām*[1] at the Dome of the Rock in Jerusalem and ending it at Tabuk [on the Arabian peninsula] with trust-in-God. It is said that on the last Pilgrimage he saw a dog panting with thirst in the desert. He called out for anyone willing to buy the merit of seventy Pilgrimages with a drink of water. Finding a purchaser, he gave the water to the dog, saying, 'This is better than all my Pilgrimages for the Prophet has said, "For every warm-blooded creature that one serves there is a reward."'[2] (NfO 77)

Abu Sa'id Abe'l-Khair told of a Sufi in the city of Merv who never left his house. By chance one day he ventured out and went to sit in the mosque. Someone brought some food and set it before him and he began, eating up all that had been provided. When he had finished, a dog appeared and attacked the Sufi. "Dealing with me is easy," the Sufi said. "I don't mind what you do to me because I know who has sent you, and who has told you to do this. However, the others here are unaware, and I don't know if they will allow you to continue."

---

[1] The ritual garment normally worn only in Mecca for the observance of the Pilgrimage.; see *Sufi Symbolism* vol. III, p.

[2] Tradition, *Ṣaḥiḥ*, Moslem (*Šalām*, 153). Cario:1929.

After a while the muezzin came and proceeded to beat the dog vigorously with a club. The dog howled in pain. The gnostic then turned to the dog and said, "You see? I told you that I didn't mind you attacking me, although I didn't know whether the others would let you stay or not. A friend would refuse a friend nothing." (AT 266)

Abo'l-Ḥasan Dailami recounted, 'Only three times have I seen my master Abu 'Abdo'llāh ebn Khafif get angry and speak harshly to someone. The first time was when the king ordered all the dogs in the city to be killed. The people then attacked the dogs, hunting them down and killing them. One dog ran into the Master's mosque, followed by a man trying to slay it. Ebn Khafif became angry and said to the man, "Stop what you are doing! Otherwise, I will make a totally sincere prostration and not a man among you will survive!" At this, fear struck the man's heart and he threw himself at the Master's feet. The man was a soldier, and repented from that profession and became a Sufi. (SKS 30)

Ḥakim Moḥammad Termedhi had nothing in the world but a hut with no door. Once when he returned from a trip to Mecca, he found that a dog had wandered into his hut and given birth to four puppies. Not wanting to put them out, the sage paced back and forth in front of the hut, hoping that the dog would take the puppies out of its own accord. (TA 527)

Shaikh Nafiso'd-Din Siwāsi told the following story: "One day Rumi asked me to buy two dirhams-worth of fine food for him at a time when a whole tray of such food cost but a single dirham. This I did immediately. He then took the food from me, wrapped it in a cloth and went out. I followed him to a derelict site, where I saw that a dog was lying with a litter of puppies. I watched, confounded by his kindness and compassion, as he gave all the food to the dog. He then said to me, 'This poor creature has had nothing to eat for a whole week. She is unable to forage because of her puppies. God heard her appeal and commanded me to look after her.' " (MAr I 377)

A dog suspected of having leprosy was thrown out of the city by the people. Aḥmad Refā'i saw this and carried the dog to a peaceful place , prepared a shelter for it, and spent forty days looking after it, until it recovered, whereupon he returned to the city. Several ignorant disciples of his protested, saying, "Why did you devote so much care and attention to a dog?" He replied, "I was afraid that the Lord would rebuke me on the Day of Resurrection, and ask, 'Why did you not take pity on that poor, sick dog?" (Anon.)

If Majnun loved the dog in Lailā's lane, the love was not for the dog but for Lailā herself. Have you not heard this verse?

One day Majnun saw a dog on the plain
and was overcome with happiness.
Asked why the dog made him happy, he replied,
"One day I saw it pass Lailā's lane." (T 139)

Bāyazid was said to have made seventy Pilgrimages, always undertaking them on foot. In the course of one of them, he came upon a group of thirsty travellers gathered near a well. He noticed that a dog was lying near the well and that the pilgrims were refusing to give it water. The dog looked up at Bāyazid and he was suddenly inspired to fetch water for it. He called out to the pilgrims, asking, "Who will buy the merit of a valid and blessed Pilgrimage for a drink of water?" No one responded. He then added five valid Pilgrimages and gradually raised the offer to the full seventy, until someone finally agreed to it. Bāyazid then thought to himself, "What a fine thing I have done, selling the merit of seventy Pilgrimages to give a dog a drink of water." When he received the water, he placed it before the dog. The dog shook its head and refused it. At this, Bāyazid fell on his face and repented. A voice then came to him, exclaiming, "How long will you go on saying 'I did this or I did that for God.' Can you not see that even a dog does not accept this?" Upon hearing this rebuke, Bāyazid cried, "I repent! I shall never think like this again!" At this the dog began to drink the water. (MAr II 670)

Arriving at a cultivated area, 'Abdo'llāh ebn Ja'far came upon a date orchard which was being worked by a slave. When the slave stopped for lunch, a dog approached him and the slave gave it a piece of bread, which the dog ate. He gave it three more pieces and the dog ate them as well. Seeing all this, 'Abdo'llāh finally asked the slave how much food he was given each day. The slave replied, "Just what you have seen." 'Abdo'llāh then asked why he had given it all to the dog and the slave replied, "There are no dogs around here. This one had to come a long distance to get here; so he must be hungry. I felt it was wrong not to feed him." 'Abdo'llāh then asked what he would eat himself. The slave replied, "I will do without today."

"I am condemned for being too generous," 'Abdo'llāh exclaimed, "but this slave is more generous than I." At this, he bought the slave and all the land that he was working, freed the slave and gave him the land. (RQ 408)

A muezzin gave the call to prayer, and Nuri cried, "What a noise! What deadly poison!" A dog barked and he responded by saying "At your service! My good fortune is with you!" The people protested that this was sacrilege, to deride the muezzin's call while responding in such a way to the bark of a dog. When they asked for an explanation, he said, "When that man was calling God's name, he was being heedless of God, and so I protested. When the dog barked it was crying '*Allāh! Allāh!*'" (RQ 425)

It is reported that a Sufi once challenged the Sufi master, Shaikh Nāṣeḥo'd-Din, on the subject of his pet dog, Qetmir, asking why he was so attached to it and enumerating the faults of dogs. The shaikh replied that he loved the dog because of its capacity for friendship with God, because it knew friend from foe and because it could distinguish between a lover and a repudiator of God. The Sufi said, "I do not agree. This is impossible." The shaikh replied, "These are the qualities that the dog of the Companions of the Cave[1] possessed. Dogs have always had these qualities. They are no different today from what they were then."

The Sufi asked how this could be proven. The shaikh replied, "It is simple. If you were to offer him the tastiest of morsels he would refuse them, whereas if I offer him but a dry crust from my hand, he will accept." Upon hearing this, the Sufi took out two dirhams and ordered the finest food to be brought and placed before Qetmir. By God's might, the dog gave it no more that a sniff and turned away, taking no further notice of it. The shaikh then produced an old crust and presented it to Qetmir, who snapped it up with the utmost eagerness and devoured it completely. At this, the Sufi abandoned his pride and spite, exercised devotion, and became detached from the world. Shaikh Nāṣeḥo'd-Din bestowed his cloak upon the Sufi who later became a disciple of Ḥosāmo'd-Din Chalabi. Before he accepted the man as his disciple, Chalabi said, "Our dogs are also masters. Imagine then what our lions must be!" (MAr II 940)

[1] Referring to Koran XVIII: 18 &19.

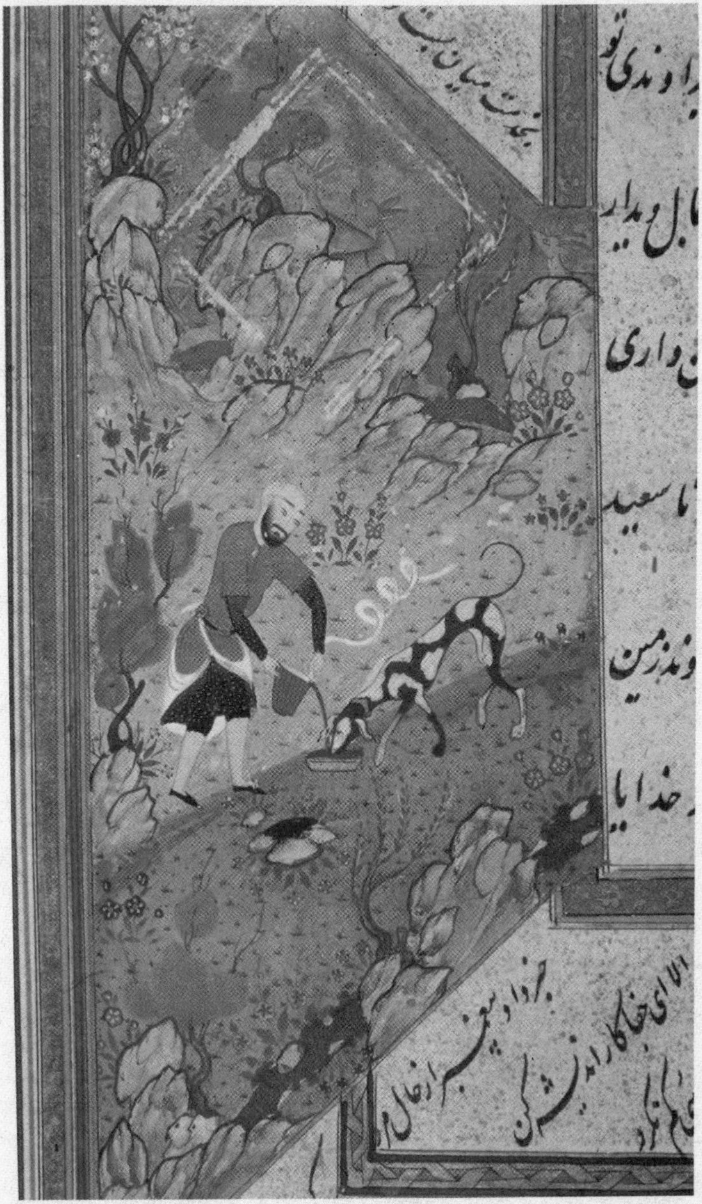

Plate 2:

A thirsty dog being given water by a man in the desert, illustrating a story in the *Bustan* of Sa'di, contained in a larger manuscript of the *Kulliyat* of Sa'di, dated 1566. The miniatures in this manuscript are done in the Shirazi Safavid style. (Add. 24944, f. 37a, B.L. London.)

Auḥado'd-Din Kermāni was sitting quietly one day when certain dismal souls, abandoned by God, came up and reviled him, saying, "You dog! You donkey of a poor excuse for a man!" Auḥado'd-Din announced that he would pay a gold dinar for every insult he might receive. His companions protested that such persons should be harassed, beaten, even killed. However, Auḥado'd-Din stipulated that the gold should be given, saying, "You do not understand! Such people are praising me, lauding and glorifying me!" "How so?" they asked. The Shaikh replied, "The one who calls me a dog is saying, 'O faithful one!' and 'O guardian of his master's gate!' And one who calls me a donkey is saying, 'O bearer of burdens!' and 'O forbearing one!' All this is praise of my qualities, not insults. The people who say these things must be protected and given the fondest care." (MAr 19)

A man encountered a dog in the desert who was so thirsty that it was barely clinging to life. There being a well nearby, this man of meritorious practise made his cap a bucket and tied his turban to it to act as a rope. He readied himself and drew a draught of water for the helpless dog. Subsequently, word came from the Prophet that God was forgiving the man's sins.

If you have been heedless, be mindful. Be devoted and practice generosity. God does not abandon one who does good for a dog; how then could one who does good for a worthy human be lost? Be as generous as you possibly can. The Keeper of the world never closes the door to blessings on anyone. (B 606)

A man, in the presence of others, boldly asked Khwāja Jondi, "Which is better, you or a dog." The disciples of Jondi immediately approached to tear the man to bits. The master stopped them and said to the man, "I am not aware of God's ordainment. My state is not known to me, my son. How can I answer you in words? If I am able to save my faith from the bandits on the Path, then I can say I am better than a dog. But if I am unable to save it from these bandits, I can only wish that I were as worthy as a single hair on a dog. Since God's purpose has not been revealed, do not value yourself by so much as a hair more than a dog. Though the dog lives in the dust of the earth, his origins are the same as yours." (EN 45)

Ma'shuq Ṭusi once absentmindedly wandered out onto the road at the hottest part of the day. A dog came along the road in his direction and Ma'shuq, without thinking, suddenly threw a stone at it. A horseman, dressed in green and with a radiant face, saw this and rode up to him. He gave Ma'shuq a lash with his whip and cried, "Hey there, heedless one! You don't know at whom you are throwing stones. In origin you are no different from this dog. After all, you are both cast from the same mold; how then can you consider him less than you? Since you are equally subject to God's power, there is no point in seeking to dominate him. Dogs are hidden behind the veil, O friend. If your reflection is pure, see beyond the flesh, where, despite an unappealing exterior, the dog is exalted in attributes. Though his outward appearance would seem to deny it, he partakes of many mysteries." (EN 46)

While walking along a road, a Sufi suddenly struck a dog by the roadside with his staff. Its paw badly wounded, the dog howled and fled. It came yelping to Abu Sa'id and fell to the ground, its heart raging at the cruelty visited upon it. It showed its paw to Abu Sa'id, who rose and summoned the offending Sufi. When he was brought before him, Abu Sa'id said, "O impure man, how could anyone be so cruel to such a helpless creature? You have smashed the dog's paw and crippled it, making it so helpless that it has collapsed."

"O master," said the Sufi, "it was not my fault, but the dog's. Since he had made my clothes ritually impure, I hit him with my staff with good reason." At this, the dog became visibly disturbed, whining in protest. Abu Sa'id then said to the dog, "By my soul, I will give you whatever makes you happy in order to make up for this. Tell me what to do now; do not leave it to the Day of Judgement. If you prefer that I deal with this man, I shall punish him on your account. I do not want you to be angry; I want you to be content." The dog then said, "O peerless one! When I saw that this man was wearing Sufi clothes, I felt sure that he would not hurt me. Little did I know that my paw would be crushed! If it had been someone dressed in ordinary clothes coming along the road, I would have kept well away from him. But because I saw him in the Sufi dress I felt confident. I was not aware of the full situation. If you are going to punish him, then do it now and strip him of the Sufi garment of kindness so that we may be forewarned of his evil, for I have never seen such harm done by a Sufi. Strip him of the Sufi cloak; that will be punishment enough for him till the Day of Judgement."

Since the dog enjoys such a station on the Path, it is a sacrilege to seek superiority over him. If you think you are higher than him, you may be sure that you are so only in your own 'dog-ness'. O man! Since you are brought to earth so wretched, you must always be humble and meek, for when you behave with arrogance, without question you will be struck down. What is there in a handful of earth that you should be so boastful? You were born only to die and to be consigned to the earth. You can be sure that the closer to the earth a person is materially, the purer he is spiritually. In making themselves like the earth, men purify body and soul in manliness. The eminent of this Path are lofty, because they have utterly rid themselves of loftiness. (EN 46)

A sincere man of religious commitment went to the mosque one evening resolving to devote the entire night to prayer. When it had grown dark, he heard a noise; it seemed that someone had entered the mosque. It occurred to the man of prayer that it might be a perfect one who resolves problems of the Path. In his heart he said, "Such a person would come to such a place solely to worship God. Without question he is aware of me. He is listening to my prayers and devotions. I must take care in my prayers so that this man will know that I am spiritually aware." He then pursued his devotions till daybreak, not letting up for even a moment. He wept freely in invoking God, at times repenting, at times begging forgiveness. He observed all the proprieties and rituals; indeed, he presented himself in fine style! When first light turned to proper dawn casting its light into the mosque, the man opened his eyes to find a dog asleep in the mosque's confines. He was so shocked that his blood boiled; tears poured over his lashes like rain. His heart so burned with shame that its gasping seared his tongue and mouth. He said to himself, "Look, you graceless man! God chastised you last night through this dog. You were active all night for the sake of the dog; have you ever stayed up all night like that for God? I have never seen you consecrate a night to worshipping God with such sincerity! Many a dog is better than you, you hypocrite! See the difference between you and a dog: Out of shamelessness you were steeped in your hypocrisy. Indeed, have you no shame before God. Now that the veil has been lifted, what are you going to say to your God? Now that I've seen what my faith has been founded on, I've lost all hope in my efforts. I'll probably never be able to do anything in the world; and if I am able to do anything, it will be only as much as a dog can do."

O man! Why do you want to rival the Devil, being stupid because of your 'dog-like' nafs? Escape this oppression of the Devil's den; flee this prison fraught with stupidity! What do you want of the imposters here? What do you seek of those who pose as guides here? Hostility towards you comes from your friends, but it is no more than a thorn from the rose-garden.

Many an imposter presents himself as a guide, being drunk with hallucination. How long are you going to pursue the imposter with his wizardry? Has the time not come for you to accept advice at last? If by the end of time one has, through this defectiveness, taken seven steps in pursuit of the imposter, according to the Prophet, one will never for an instant be able to free oneself from him. One will be an adherent of the impostor in all states; one will remain eternally a follower of the imposter. This is what happens to one who takes seven steps against religion in pursuit of the imposter: If someone is motivated by deceit and deception for seventy years and follows in the footsteps of the imposter, Eblis, I wonder what his state is going to be.

Since your imposters are the deceitful Devil, the world and the oppressive *nafs*, how can one with all these rebellious imposters be happy for a moment! Many a one with a guided heart and virtuous behavior has become entangled with this imposter of the world. Much blood has this imposter shed, not just one day, but for tens of thousands of years! (EN 72)

The Prophet told of a woman who was considered to be a transgressor. While proceeding in the desert, she came upon a well by which was standing a dog, panting with thirst. Moved by pity, she abandoned her work, made a bucket of her shoe and a rope of her head-covering to draw water for the dog. For this God blessed her in both His worlds. The Prophet said that on his *me'rāj* [Journey of ascent] he saw her, radiant as the moon, with the whole paradise of Eden at her disposal.[1]

When the transgressor gave water to the dog, her reward from God was that of merit many times over. If you bring peace for but a moment to a heart, the merit therefrom cannot be compared with the two worlds. This is because the heart is without self and the merit therefrom goes beyond even the two worlds. Self-ness is loss; become selfless with aspiration *(hemmat)*, so that through selflessness you may attain exaltation. (EN 294)

Someone once asked Shebli, who had first motivated him on the Path towards God. Shebli answered, "I saw a dog by the roadside, beside itself with thirst. There was a puddle in the road; yet every time the dog approached it, it saw its own image therein and leapt back in terror, thinking that it was another dog. Fear of the other dog prevented it from drinking. Finally, the dog became so desperate that it could no longer contain its thirst and leapt into the water, whereupon the other dog disappeared. When the dog was no longer before his own eyes, it became clear that the dog himself was his own vice. This taught me that I myself was the veil before myself. I became annihilated from myself and was successful. Thus it was a dog who was my first

[1] Bokhāri, *Jāme' aṣ-ṣaḥiḥ. (Bad' al-khalq. 17)*. Cairo:1956-7.

teacher on the Path."

You, too, arise from before your own eyes; you are your own veil; arise from in front of yourself. If there is the least hair of self in the way, you will have to deal with a severe attachment. It would have been better for you, you feeble old man, if they had taken you straight from the cradle to the coffin! The foundation that God gave Moses was due to his having set out from the cradle in a casket. If God's presence is to be continuous for you, do not bring your self along. It is sufficient for you to become selfless, divorced from yourself, to where this selflessness is 'light upon light.' (XXXIV, 35) (EN 155)

A dog dropped dead and lay by the roadside; death brought its teeth into prominence. By the time Jesus, son of Mary, happened upon the carcass, it was already emitting a bad stench. He said to a companion, "He is God's own; look at the whiteness of his teeth!" Jesus sensed neither ugliness nor odor; whatever others thought ugly, he saw as beauty. Accustom yourself to seeing purely if you are a devotee of God; see only purity if you are a devotee with insight.

See everything in one shade and one measure; see the snake as a 'snake stone';[1] do not see the snake stone as a snake. Choose to see beauty and virtue; choose to exercise

[1] A sometimes snake-shaped and snake-colored substance that forms in the intestines of animals and is traditionally used as an antidote for snake bite.

حکایت
در صفت کرکس مردار خوار

Plate 3:

The story of Jesus and the dead dog. In the *Makhzan al-asrār*, by Niẓāmi. This book is contained within a larger manuscript of a *Khamseh,* dated 1664-7. The miniature is signed by the Turkoman artist Ṭālib Lālā of the Du'l-qadir tribe, done in the Isfahan style during the Safavid period. (Add. 6631, f.19b, B.L., London.)

kindness and faithfulness. If you know God, be a devotee, and be grateful for God's bounty. You are receiving this bounty all the time, but you are not grateful for it. (MN 302)

One morning a munificent king gave food to wretched Bohlul, who, in turn, gave it to a dog, who ate it. Someone rebuked him saying, "Who would ever do such a thing? You have no respect for such a king that you give his food to dogs. Such disrespect is criminal; disrespectful behavior is unacceptable."

"Hush, O empty-headed one!" Bohlul told him. "If dogs only knew that the food was the king's, God knows, they would be so ashamed about eating it that they wouldn't do so, even if their lives depended on it!" (MN.114)

There was once a spiritual leader, a guide, who sought one day a guest from God. "O Lord of the World," he said in his heart, "may a guest come from You tomorrow morning." The following day he made preparation for his guest. Keeping a lookout in all directions, he spotted a helpless dog coming down the road. The man abjectly drove away the dog, his heart still eager in expectation of the hoped-for guest's eventual arrival, that God's gift might all the sooner appear. Despite all his expectations, no one came into view on the road; finally, the agitated host fell asleep.

"O self-confounded one," said God in a dream, "I sent along a dog as one of My own, so that you might make him your guest, but you sent him away, so that he went off hungry and resentful of you." The man woke up at this, confused, feverish, and drenched in tears. He dashed around in all directions, until at last he found the dog off in a corner. Going up to the creature, he burst into tears, begging forgiveness and explaining everything.

"O man of the Path," said the dog, "you asked for a guest, but first you should have asked for insight from God. If you want to receive a guest from God, you must have insight, for if God grants you a grain of insight, your measure will be that of a hundred thousand years-worth. If you have no insight, ask it of God, for you cannot travel the Path without it." (MN 137)

From the hut of a ragged gnostic, the sound of a dog's bark reached the ears of a passerby. He asked himself what a dog would be doing in such a place and entered the hut in search of the righteous gnostic. He saw the gnostic but no sign of a dog. Embarrassed, he began to back out, being too ashamed to bring up this thing that was puzzling him. The gnostic heard the man's footsteps and called out,

35

Plate 4:

A man drinking wine while feeding meat to a dog, being an example of a *Sharabhanga*, a kind of ascetic who rejects the ordinary ideas concerning pollution. This miniature is one of the illustrations in the *Tashrih al-akhvām*, which is an account of the origins of some of the different occupations, sects and tribes. It is done in the Mughal style and dated 1825. (Add 27255, f. 374, B.L., London.)

"Why are you standing by the door? Come in! Don't think, my dear friend, that there's a dog barking here; the sound came from me. When I saw that God likes abjectness, I cast off pride and rational opinion. I set about barking like a dog by God's door, for I could conceive of no one more wretched than a dog."

If you wish to advance in value, you must climb the steep slope of humility. On this plane those who have humbled themselves the most come out foremost. When a flood sweeps in bringing terror and dread, those whose heads are lofty with pride fall low. But when dew humbly falls from the flower the heavens bear it with kindness up to the Pleiades." (B 324)

I have heard that Jonaid once saw a dog on the plain of San'ā', its teeth for tearing prey having fallen out. Its claws, having once had the power to seize lions, were now useless, like those of a feeble old fox. Once it had chased deer and mountain sheep; now it took kicks from the nomads' sheep. Seeing it wretched, beaten and bruised, Jonaid gave it half his provisions.

Jonaid broke down and wept, saying, "Who knows which of us is better? It would seem that today I am the better, but God knows what fate has planned for me! If the foot of my faith does not slip, I may earn the crown of God's forgiveness for my head. If I do not keep the dress of gnosis on, I shall be lower than many a dog. For all the bad name that the dog has been given, when it dies, it will not go to hell."

The way of the Path, Sa'di, is this: The men of the Path did not see themselves as great. They were more exalted than the angels because they considered themselves no better than dogs. (B 328)

A dog once found a cake in the road; then suddenly he noticed the moon. Dropping the cake, he dashed off to seize the moon from the sky. As fast as he ran, he could not catch the moon, so he went back to the roadside in search of the cake. Try as he might, he could not find it, so he rushed off again in pursuit of the moon. However much he traveled the length and breadth of the road, he had neither the cake in hand nor the moon. In dismay he stood in the middle of the road, lost, having failed to possess either.

Unless you have experienced such pain in your heart, you have not experienced life. You must experience pain at every moment, not a little, but as much as worlds upon worlds, so that this pain will advance you along the Path, and take you to God, without yourself. (MN 154)

Someone asked a dog, "O you who are content with one or two crumbs from the world, who have experienced both favour and hardship from the world, who have known both good and bad from people, how can you tell a kindly person from a cruel one?" The dog replied, "When I am traveling along, cruelty will strike arbitrarily. Sticks and stones can come from any direction; sometimes it's a stick, sometimes a stone." (HAu 101)

A pious man dwelled in a cave on Mount Lebanon, isolated from the world like the sleepers of the Cave.[1] He had turned the face of his heart from what is other than God; his seclusion had brought him the boon of exaltation. He spent his days fasting and received a loaf of bread each night. Half the loaf served as his supper and half his breakfast, and a hundred joys swelled in his heart from contentment. His life went on in this manner, such that he never came down from the mountain.

It so happened that one evening the loaf did not arrive and this godly man grew weak and frail from hunger. He did his evening prayers; then came time for his night ones; his heart was tempted by thoughts of dinner. The pious man was so disturbed about his meal that he neither observed his nightly devotional practice nor slept. When morning came, he descended from that serene station for the sake of a little food.

[1] The main subject of Sura XVIII, known as 'The Companions of the Cave.'

There was a village at the foot of the mountain, the inhabitants of which were all heathens and villains. The pious man went and stood by the door of a heathen, who gave him a couple of barley loaves. Taking the bread, he thanked him; he was happy to receive food and joyfully set off for the cave to break his fast with the barley bread.

In the heathen's house there was a wolf-like dog, who was nothing but skin and bones from starvation. If you were to draw a circle with a compass before him, he would see it as a round loaf and die with delight. If one were to mention the word 'breath' he would hear it as bread and fall down faint. That dog, then began sniffing after the pious man, coming up to him and tugging at his garment. The pious man threw him a loaf, then went away to avoid any trouble. The dog gobbled the bread down and came after him to harrass him again. The pious man gave him the other bread straightaway, so that the dog would stop bothering him. The dog ate the bread and ran straight after the man without looking back. Sticking to him like a shadow, he barked and tore his clothing.

When the pious man saw what was happening, he cried, "I have never seen a dog like you, so shameless! Your master gave me only two loaves of barley-bread, and you took those two loaves from me, you wretched beast! Now, what are you running after me for? And why do you keep tearing my clothes?"

"O perfect one," the dog replied, "I am not shameless! Rub your eyes! Ever since I was little, my home has been this old heathen's hut. I herd his sheep and guard his house. Once in a while, he gives me half a loaf, occasionally a few bones. Many times he simply forgets to feed me, and this heedlessness gives me a bitter taste. Many a morn and eve I have seen no bread, met with no food. Weeks may go by when I am helpless and I see no sign of either bread or bone. Sometimes the poor old man finds no bread for himself, let alone me. Since I was raised

در ساعد پوشند

Plate 5:

A dog greeting his master. From the *Miftāḥ al Foḍhalā* by Moḥammad Ebn Maḥmud Shādiyābādi, (a glossary of rare words and proper names according to ancient Persian poetry). The miniatures in this manuscript are in the Persian style dating from the 15th century. This picture illustrates the entry for the word *dumbāleh* (tail wagging). (Or. 3299, f.128, B.L. London.)

in his household, I have not considered any other. My work is by the door of this old heathen; sometimes I receive and am grateful; sometimes I must be patient.

When I fell in love with him, I knew no other door but his. Although sometimes he takes a stick and beats me and sometimes throws stones I will not leave his door. When one night your bread did not reach you, it smashed the foundations of your endurance. You forsook the door of the Provider and rushed straight to that of a heathen. You abandoned the Friend for a loaf of bread, coming to terms with His enemy. Be fair now, O Divinely favored man; who is the more shameless: I or you? Be objective."

The pious man was dumbfounded by these words; he slapped his head and fell faint. O dog of my *nafs*, learn contentment from the dog of that old heathen! (Shaikh Bahā'i)

A dog was dying, and its owner, a Bedouin was sobbing, shedding tears, and crying in sorrow. "What am I to do with myself? What is to be done? Henceforth, how can I live without you?"

A beggar passed by and asked, "What is this sobbing? For whom is your mourning and lamentation?"

The Bedouin replied, "There was in my possession a dog of excellent disposition. But look now, he is dying on the road. He hunted for me by day and kept watch by night; he was a lion, my servant, not a dog. He was keen-eyed and good at catching my enemies and driving off thieves. He was good-natured, faithful and kind."

The beggar asked, "What ails him? Has he been wounded?" The bedouin replied, "Ravenous hunger has made him so lamentable."

"Show some patience," said the beggar, "in bearing this pain and anguish; the grace of God bestows a recompense on those who are patient." Then he asked the Bedouin, "O noble chief, what is this full bag in your hand?"

The Bedouin replied, "Food left over from last night, which I am taking along with me to nourish myself."

"Why don't you give some to the dog?" asked the beggar.

"I have not love and liberality to this extent," replied the Bedouin. "Bread cannot be obtained by a traveler on the road without money, but water from the eyes costs nothing."

At this the beggar cried, 'Shame on you, O water-skin full of wind! For in your opinion a crust of bread is better than tears." (MM V 477-487)

A beggar, whose all and everything was a dog who was constantly by his side, was told, "Look, my good old man, don't keep losing face by being accompanied by this dog. You who eat at the expense of others, why persist in suffering because of your beast?"

When he heard this, the poor beleaguered old man could only reply, "If I were to drive away this comrade of mine, then who would I have for a friend?"[1]

[1] Written by the author at sixteen, before entering the world of Sufism.

PART II

VIRTUOUS QUALITIES OF DOGS

The following are stories told by the Sufis praising the virtuous qualities of dogs.

If humanity means merely to have human form, Moḥammad and his antagonist Abu Jahl would be just the same. Moḥammad and Abu Jahl both went to the idol-temple but there's a world of difference between the former's entry therein and that of the latter. Abu Jahl bowed to the idols as an idol worshipper while the idols bowed to Moḥammad.

The portrait of Adam looks like Adam; see from the pictured form what thing in it is wanting. The soul is wanting in that lifeless form: go, seek that rare jewel! The heads of all the lions in the world were laid low when God bestowed favor on the dog of the Companions of the Cave.

What does it matter if that dog had such a despised appearance, if its soul was plunged in the ocean of light? The pen itself does not contain the description of outward forms. It is only when written that the qualities of words like learned and just may be distinguished; the qualities of learning and justice are spiritual essences which you will not find in any place. (MM I 1019-1025)

Majnun, like a ship that was destined to be wrecked, sat on a broken plank. Since the power of yearning had borne him, like a steed, to the land of that faithful one, Lailā. He searched frantically about in all directions, seeking an indication of his beloved.

Suddenly he saw a dog in the distance, which had collapsed; its running days were over. Its foreleg tendons had gone slack and its claws had lost their grip for prey. Mange had caused the dog's hair to fall out and its face was ravaged with wounds inflicted by wild beasts. The dog was so emaciated that the bones could be seen through the flesh. This dog looked more like a bag of bones — or a quiver full of arrows. Its hairless tail was looped like a coiled snake. It had no teeth to chew bones with. At one point when starvation had threatened its life, it seems that it had gnawed away its teeth, as if they themselves were bones. The dog whined in pain from the sores on its flanks caused by malnutrition. Each sore was like a mouth in its skin with a tongue poking through, proclaiming the dog's fidelity.

The white of the underlying bones appeared like teeth in

خم یافته در تهی کشش راه
تشنه شکمش همه تهیگاه

از دم دهنش فراز مانده
دندانش ز خنده باز مانده

سرتا قدمش جراحت و ریش
شویان زبان جراحت خویش

بی لقمه گلوی لقمه خوارش
لیسیدن دست و پای کارش

خویشان که ز خویش سیر گردند
لختی بکشش دلیر کردند

کوشند اگرچه در جدایی
زینسان نبرند آشنایی

بنمای رخ این چه روی تافتست
بیدار شو ای چه دیر خوابست

گر بنگری این تن خرابم
باری رخ خود نما بخوابم

از خواب تو در برادران تاب
خوش خفته تو با برادران خواب

Plate: 6

Majnun fondling Lailā's dog in the desert, when visited by an old man whom his father had sent. This is an illustration for Niẓām's *Mathnawi Lailā va-Majnun* which is contained within a larger manuscript, a *Khamseh* dating from the late 16th century Safavid period, done in the Qazvini style. (Or. 11326, f. 11b, B.L., London.)

those mouth-like sores — No, rather, the skin on its body gushed with more than a hundred wellsprings forming traps, whereby, instead of the dog hunting prey, those wellsprings drew flies in search of their sustenance.

A fox kept strutting by, taunting him, "Arise, O panther-catching lion; come match wits with the weary-hearted fox! How long are you going to sleep naked on the ground wherever you go? Come, get yourself a pelt!"

When Majnun saw the dog's appearance, he ran over to it, with tears streaming forth. He fell, like a shadow, at its feet, kissing the ground beneath them. He wiped its paws with the moisture of his eyes and spread smooth pebbles as a bed for it. He made of his lap a pillow for its head, sheltering it in the shade of his kindness. He washed its sores with the tears of his eyes and soothed the itching of its body with a gentle hand. He brushed the dust from its head and face and drove the flies from its back and flanks.

When he had finished his comforting the dog, he began to speak in a caressing tone: "O you with the collar of fidelity and before whom lions have prostrated. You are better than a man in terms of fidelity and more intimate with the Way than most. If you eat once from someone's hand, a hundred stones will not make you turn your back on him.

Your work is to keep watch by night, and your practice to tend the sheep by day. You make the thief lose his taste for his trade and imprison the wolf in your lion-like claws. Your bark frightens away night-travelers, while guards are frozen in fear. On the battlefield of the righteous, one hair of yours is equal to that of a thousand armed men. When you charge in courageously, your lion-like boldness makes an armed man less than a dog.

Many who have lost their way in the dark of the night have been guided to their home by the sound of your bark. For someone lost at night, your bark is like the warm strains of an organ; and because it comes from Lailā's lane, it relieves the burdens of the soul. When you go out hunting, the King of the world is watching out for you. Your leash will be in His hand and it is up to him when to fasten it or release it. Your raiment will be of lustrous silk, your collar of gold, encrusted with jewels. If He falls back from among those who travel with you, He will drive his steed on to catch up with you. He will entrust your affairs to His own care and give you your own banquet spread.

When He releases you to chase the prey, you can never err in the chase. So bent are you on running swiftly that your very shadow is left behind. Whether fowl or even the wind is your intended prey, it can never escape. Many a swift and seasoned fox whose hide has been slashed by your wounding blows, in seeking to have it mended the same day, has gone on to the shop of the Mender of Pelts. Anticipating the pain you inflict, the panther flees the power of your paw, and even with his agility and power he still seeks refuge from you at the top of a mountain. Having heard of your cunning and stratagems, the lion slinks away into the cane-brake. Even with all those bristling spears of cane, clustered round, he still refuses to fight with you! What chance has a deer against your strength, when even an elk is no match for it? No wild ass who is wounded by you is able to escape alive. If a rabbit ever sees you in a dream, he will never sleep again. This is the tale of your youth, the history of the purity of your life." (HAu 875)

Majnun was once seen petting a dog and kissing it, melting with fondness before it; he was pacing round it, stooping humbly in circumambulation, exactly like a pilgrim round the Ka'ba. He kissed the dog's head and paws and navel; and he gave it

" It is the dog of blessed countenance, the dog of my cave. It is the sharer of my grief and woe. The dust of the paws of the dog who has become a resident of her lane is better than mighty lions. How should I give a single hair of that dog who stays in her lane to the lions? Oh, since the lions are devoted slaves to her dogs, there is no possibility of speaking further. Silence, and farewell!"

If you pass beyond form, O friends, it is Paradise and rose-gardens within rose-gardens. (MM I 567-578)

O You Whose eye of grace is open to all those who turn to You in need! Lovers become fervent over You; their hearts burn in desiring You! Pain for You at every moment is their intimate companion; burning unsoothed is their soothing salve. Delivered from themselves through worship of You, they have become ennobled through bondsmanship to You. They wear the cloak of poverty and annihilation, and they strive in the way of sincerity and purity.

Their necks arch proudly, for they wear the dog's collar and they run in the way of fidelity. Jāmi, who is their dog, like them, adheres to the cult of fidelity. I have been caught by Your lasso! Do not deprive me of the brand which marks your dogs.

I have my eye closed to the banquet of riches. Place a bone of poverty before me. Make patience, poverty and annihilation my practice; sweeten the bitterness of patience for me. (HAu 495)

Who am I? What have I done to be equal to Your lovers? Honor for me is to kiss the feet of Your servants.

Hoping from the banquet, for but a splinter of bone which is worthy of the Simorgh alone. I lay my head like the dog, each night on Your threshold, to keep my rivals from begging at your door. ('Erāqi)

Ever since your dogs have become my friends,
I have become a stranger
to my family and friends. (Jāmi)

If you want to be somebody, be his slave.
If you become his dog, that is already a lot. (MN 297)

Call me dog, but do not drive me away from that threshold, for a single bone is enough for me in your lane.

If I find a bone from your lane, I shall spread a banquet before the Simorgh of fortune. (EN 302)

O Kamāl! See the lofty aspiration of that dog of
His lane,
Who is ashamed to be my companion and friend.
(Kamāl Khojandi)

As the following passages demonstrate, the dog is considered to be a model for fidelity in Sufi literature.

The dog is better than that person who brings distress to the heart of his friends. One should dwell on the truth of these words, until the meaning thereof sinks into one's heart.

A man shares your table; the dog is banned and stands by your threshold. What a shame that the dog is faithful, while a man bites the hand that feeds him! (Sa'di)

If we turn away from your lane,
Then the dog, in his fidelity, is better than us.
('Aṭṭār)

A dog never forgets one gave it a bite to eat even if it is stoned a hundred times, whereas if you pamper a base person all his life, the slightest harshness will make him your enemy.(G 589)

I am the dog at the threshold of neediness,
My collar is fashioned from fidelity to God.
(Jāmi)

God bestowed upon the people of Sabā much ease, myriads of castles, palaces and orchards. But those ill-humored ones rendered no thanks for that bounty; in fidelity they were less than dogs.

When a dog is given piece of bread from a particular house, he will give his allegiance to that house. He will become the watcher and guardian of that door, even though violence and ill-treatment befall him. Still he will not budge from that door; he would consider it ingratitude to prefer another.

Again, if a strange dog comes by day or night to a quarter of the town, the dogs there will at once teach him a lesson, saying, "Begone to the place that is your first lodging: indebtedness for that kindness is the heart's pledge, which it must redeem." They will bite him, saying, "Return to your place, do not leave the debt of that kindness unpaid any longer."

From the door of the friend and from the hand of the people of heart, how much have you drunk the water of life, and your eyes were opened! Then how much have you fed your spirit with the food of mystical intoxication, ecstasy and selflessness at the door of the people of heart? Then, through greed, you abandoned that door, and now because of your deceit you are going round to every shop. (MM III 285-95)

خواست تا سنگی بردارد و سگ را دفع کند زمین یخ گرفته
بود و میسر نشد عاجز ماند گفت انیچه حرام زاده قومند که

سگ را گشاده اند و سنگ را بسته امیر از غرفه بدید و بشنید
و بخندید و گفت از من خیری بخواه گفت جامه خود میخواهم

Plate 7:

An illustration for a tale from the *Golestan* by Sa'di about a poet who visits the house of a band of robbers, hoping to be given a few dirhams for his verses. The owner of the house was not happy with his poem. He had the poet stripped of his robe and sent on his way. The owner's dog chased after him as he fled. The poet tried to pick up a stone to throw at the dog in order to hinder its pursuit but he found the stones frozen to the ground. The poet cried out "What kind of bastards are these who let their dogs free but tie their stones to the ground?" His host on hearing the poet's remark laughed and told him to ask a favor of him. The poet answered, "I only ask for my own cloak." The style of the miniature is Mughal. It dates from the early 19th century. (Or. 349, f. 86b, B.L., London.)

The Sufis in their writings have used the dog's capacity to be trained as an example to be followed by others Sufis. The following passages will illustrate this parallel.

Examples of dogs that are instructed and trained are the hunting and sheep dogs:

When the dog has learned the knowledge imparted to him, he has escaped from error; he hunts only lawful prey in the bush. (MM II 2363)

A body ruled by the passions is no better than a dog, and likewise spiritual endeavor (*mojāhada)* and discipline are no less than the work of a dog-keeper. When a dog-keeper subjects the mischievous dog to discipline for a period of time, so that the dog becomes what is known as his master's dog, such a dog will always accompany its master whenever he goes hunting or goes out surveying for the hunt. In the field all eyes are upon the dog, watching to see what he will do. What he kills is received as living bounty, and whatever he does wrong is seen as right, and if he fails to find game, the men excuse him, while if he does find game and catches it, he is stroked by the master, and on the dog-keeper is conferred the robe of honor. For his whole life, the nobles are at his service. Whenever he is missing, he is remembered at every moment.

A dog that has undergone a brief period of discipline has gained enough knowledge to be aware of where he must go when he is sent forth, how to return when he is summoned, and how game should be caught. A dog is the most mischievous of creatures. If he experiencs a heightening of knowledge even to this minimal extent, he comes to enjoy the stroking of the ruler, fine clothes and a collar of gold. How could God, therefore, withhold the benefit of the ocean of His grace and generosity from a believer who adheres to Divine Unity (*tauḥid)* and is one of God's most precious creatures, when the believer has repented and turned away from his passions and become engaged in spiritual endeavor in knowledge and worship? The repenter deserves forgiveness, being the chosen one of the Merciful; and his heart is the object of contemplation for the God of the World. (OT 77)

Plate 8:

Detail:: A group of dogs with their keeper from a miniature in the *Nafaḥat al-ons* by Jāmi, illustrating a story about Najm al-Din Kobra, copied for Akbar at Agra, dated 1605, and signed by Madhu. (Or. 1362, f. 263a, B.L., London.)

An example of a dog experiencing love, becoming a gnostic, and acquiring a human temperament is the dog of the Companions of the Cave (Koran; Sura XVIII), as described by the Sufi poets:

For a few days the dog of the companions of the Cave
Followed the virtuous and so became human. (G 82)

Wolf, bear and lion know what love is; one who is blind to love is inferior to a dog. If the dog had not a vein of love, how could the dog of the Cave have sought to win the heart of the sleepers therein?

Moreover, in the world there are many like this, dog-like in appearance, though not as celebrated as the dog of the Cave. If you have not gotten a whiff of the heart in your own kind, how can you detect the heart in dog and sheep? (MM V 2008-2011)

When the dog has become wise, he marches briskly; when the dog has become a gnostic he becomes as the Men of the Cave. (MM II 2364)

Do not question the dog of the companions of the Cave, for he has a soul dedicated to love. (MN 235)

Step forth on the way of lovers! Why be less than a dog on the Path; for when that dog caught the scent of this Way, neither stick nor stone could turn him from the Path. (AN 130)

The Sufis in their literature have also praised the dog's sense of patience, gratitude, service and self-sacrifice.

It is said that when Shaqiq Balkhi asked Imam Ja'far Sādeq about chivalry (*fotowwat*), the latter asked him what he thought that it meant. Shaqiq said, "To be grateful when one is given something and to be patiently forbearing when something is withheld." Ja'far replied, "The dogs of our town do just that."

"O descendant of the Prophet of God!" exclaimed Shaqiq, "What then does chivalry mean to you?"

"To give to others when one is given something," replied Ja'far, "and to be patiently forbearing when nothing is forthcoming." (RQ 363)

Since I cannot be a guest at the feast of Union with you,
Let me place my head in service, let me lie like a dog at the threshold. (Jāmi)

Abu 'Othmān Maghrebi recounted: "Before I embarked on the Sufi Path, I had a horse and a dog, and used to spend my time hunting on an island. I had a wooden bowl, which I used to fill with milk. One day, when I went to drink milk from the bowl, the dog started barking furiously and attacked me the moment I picked up the bowl to drink. When I tried a second time, it jumped at me again. When I made a third attempt, the dog rushed over and, ducking its head down into the bowl, lapped up the milk. Immediately it swelled up and died. The dog had seen a snake poison the milk. It had sacrificed itself for my sake, "When I saw that, I repented and undertook the Sufi Path." (NfO 87)

Like a dog, I bark in Your lane every morning,
Yet you never ask whose dog I am or why I am here. ('Erāqi)

Plate 9:

This is an illustration for the tale of a hunter and his dog in *Makhzan al asrār,* by Niẓāmi. The dog disappears one day and the hunter, grief-stricken, manages to maintain his composure, relying on patience and reason. A fox comes on the scene. Seeing the hunter in this distraught state he berates him for his devotion to the dog, and counsels him to put the dog out of his mind. A moment later, as the picture illustrates, the hunter's dog runs up and seizes the deceptive fox. The hunter's patient faith and devotion to the dogs loyalty and service, based on his certainty and trust in Providence, allows Neẓāmi to draw this moral:

Whosesoever certitude leads him to devotion
Shall be at last befriended by good fortune
For certain, feet become heads by motion
By thought—for sure— is stone to gold transformed.

This book is contained within a larger manuscript of a Khamseh, dated 1664-7. The miniature is signed by the Turkoman artist Ṭālib Lālā of the Du'l-qadir tribe, done in the Isfahan style during the Safavid period. (Add. 6631, f.16b B.L. London.)

The trained hunting dog is respected by people, not the stray dog of the city streets:

The stray dog of the city is always subjected to stoning and torment because it is not out doing service by chasing game for the hunt. (Sa'di)

PART III

SUFI SCHOLARS' CRITICISM OF DOGS

Unlike the Sufis, for the majority of the people in the Middle East the dog represents negative characteristics. The following passages show how in some of their writings the Sufis reflected these contemporary folk customs and social mores.

In Sufi literature, the commanding soul (*nafs-e ammāra*) has been likened to a dog. This association is prompted by the Koranic verse: "And had We willed, We could have raised him by their means, but he clung to the earth and followed his own lust. Therefore his likeness is as the likeness of a dog; if thou attackest him he panteth with his tongue out, and if thou leavest him he panteth with his tongue out." (VII: 176)

From this point of view, the commanding *nafs* is like a stray dog, creating trouble, being ready to bite, whether one attacks it or leaves it alone. Alternatively, the commanding *nafs* can be compared to a stray dog concerning its irascible and savage qualities and many of its inclinations. In their writings, gnostics have compared the commanding *nafs* to a dog with this aspect in mind.

Take heed! Do not wish life to this dog-like *nafs*; it is the enemy of your spirit since long ago. (MM II 274)

Ḥallāj told his son, "Look here, my fine boy, occupy the *nafs* with something and do not let it become sated or it will turn into a lion!" (EN 246)

This rebellious *nafs* has made me wretched; night and day it has plunged me into a sad frame of mind. Spare me from this dog on the Way! Pay attention to it, so that it might become aware. (EN 313)

You have fallen low because of this miserable dog of a *nafs*; you have become drowned in pollution. That dog of hell which you've heard about sleeps within you, and you are blissfully unaware. Whatever you feed this fire-eating dog of hell, it devours with relish.

You may be sure that tomorrow this dog of a *nafs* will raise its head up out of hell as your enemy. This *nafs* is your enemy, worse than a dog; how long will you nourish this dog, O ignorant one! (MN 182)

The heart is ever a mounted huntsman in the country of the body and this dog-like *nafs* its companion day and night. No matter how fast the huntsman gallops, the dog keeps up beside him in the hunt. Whoever has the manliness to bring this dog to heel can lasso a lion in both the worlds. No man can measure up to the dust under the feet of one who subjugates this dog. Even the dust on one who performs the rare feat of putting this dog on leash is more precious than the blood of others. (MT 111)

A monk once built himself a cell, locking the door from within and making a hole in the door. He sat there for a time, engaged in devotions, practising all sorts of austerities until Abo'l-Qāsem Hamadāni passed by and walked around the cell, calling the monk; the monk however refused to come out. In the end, the master shouted so much that the monk called down from the roof, "O noisy one, why are you disturbing one as bewildered as me? What do you want with me? Tell me truly!"

"What I want," replied the master, "is for you to explain to me, if you like, what you are doing in this place."

"O master," replied the monk, "you ask me what I am doing! What do you think I'm doing? I saw a vicious dog in myself, running senselessly around the town. I have imprisoned it in this cell, closed the door on it and subjected it to discipline. This dog has attacked many people in the world, but now, in the monastery it bothers only me. I have left my wife and children to lock this dog up in a prison. You, too, should lock him up, so he won't keep bothering a bewildered soul whenever he feels like it." (EN 75)

The dog of low aspiration looks for a bone, while the lion's paw seeks the marrow of life. The man of high aspirations wants no limitation; the dog is a dog, content with a crumb. You have been endowed with high status in essence; so why, like a dog, have you such low aspiration? (HH 111)

If a dog is hit by a clod on the head, he leaps with joy that it might be a bone; and if two persons pass by carrying a bier on their shoulders with a body upon it, this ignoble creature thinks it is a banquet ready to be spread. (G 494)

A king who wanted to go hunting asked the dog-keeper to bring him a fast hunting dog. He was brought a trained dog, whose covering was of the finest satin. The king had made a jewel-studded collar, with which to honor the dog. It bore an anklet and bracelet of gold and a silken leash tied round its neck. The king considered the dog to be intelligent, taking its leash in his own hand.

The king rode ahead, the dog running behind; in the dog's path lay a bone. The dog stopped because of the bone. The king watched as the dog came to a halt.

The fire of jealousy flared so in the king that it burned that misguided dog. "Indeed," exclaimed the king, "when one is following the king, how can one look at some other thing?"

He released the leash and then ordered, "Let this gross one go out into the world!" The dog would have preferred the pain of a hundred thousand needles, to having lost that leash.

The dog-keeper said, "The dog is dressed up and covered with precious gems. This dog is only worthy of the plain and the desert. Let us take the satin gold and gems before he goes."

"Leave it be; let it go as it is," said the king. "Don't be concerned with the silver and gold that it wears. One day it might become aware, seeing itself dressed in such a way, it will recall that it was once the friend of a king and is now separated from him."

O you who have friendship in pre-eternity and then become separated through heedlessness, enter fully into True Love; drink the cup in a manly way with the dragon. True love is the battlefield of the dragons and the blood-money for lovers is in the losing of their heads. That which quickens the soul of a man reduces a dragon to the form of an ant. The King's lovers, be they one or a hundred, thirst for their own blood in His Way. (MT 126)

A pilgrim once gave me an ivory comb, for which may the character of pilgrims be blessed! I was told that once he had called me a dog because he had harbored a slight grudge against me. I threw away the comb and told the man that I did not need this bone and not to call me a dog again. When I am satisfied with my own vinegar, why should I go begging for sweets from the sweet shop?

Be content, O *nafs*, with little, so that you may see a king and a pauper as one. Why beg at the door of a king? When you cease to crave, you become a king. If you worship yourself then be a glutton and beg at every door. (B1133)

Don't approach the door of the commander, the minister, or the king, alone and without an escort. When door-keeper and dog confront a stranger, one seizes the collar, the other the skirts.(G 101)

When Shaikh Abu Sa'id Abe'l-Khair was in Nishapur, he was being repudiated by various parties, including Qoshairi. Although Qoshairi's repudiation resolved itself after attending one of Abu Sa'id's gatherings, from time to time a critical judgement about attachment to material human nature would pose itself in the scholar's heart.

One day Qoshairi was part of a group who went walking

with Abu Sa'id. A stray dog entered the lane, and the dogs of the lane raised a clamor of barking, setting upon the intruder, wounding him and driving him out. Abu Sa'id stopped and said, "I too am a stranger in this town. Do not treat me in the way these dogs have treated this stray." At that, all repudiation and critical judgment disappeared from Qoshairi's heart once and for all, and he became purified. (AT 220)

A dog was complaining of his lot to someone, "No one can see what a distressed and miserable state I am in. I have neither a nest like the birds nor grain like the ants; my characteristic is acquiescence and my practice is forbearance. I am innocently battered by thousands of stones, hurled from every direction, yet no frown appears on my brow. Who can claim the station of austerity and seclusion that I possess, I, whose bed-clothes are clods of earth and whose pillow is a stone?

"Whenever someone feeds me, I do not mind if afterwards, he beats me with a stick. If I am fed, I eat; if not I run free, not huddling in anger like human beings. I don't steal things from people like the cat; and if crumbs happen to fall my way, I scrabble for them bit by bit.

I enjoy neither the provision of winter nor the luxury of summer; this old pelt suffices me from year to year. Who could sit in my place at the station of contentment, where a rose-garden and a dung-heap are the same to me?

What have I, whose life is of this nature and whose

temperament is of this kind, done to deserve such stones and curses?"

"Talk no more about yourself," came the reply, "for any attempt to praise you on my part is confounded. These two cursed traits are enough: That I see you as a foe to the stranger and as a scavenger." (G 856)

That one of pure essence, the Prophet, has said that one who follows the world is worse than a dog, for this treacherous world is a carcass.[1]

Dogs crowd round a carcass; when one has had his full, he leaves it for another dog to take it up. He does not hoard the slightest scrap; he has not the least thought of tomorrow.

On the other hand, whoever seeks the world is constantly rolling like a polo ball in play. Like the ball, he keeps rolling along as a matter of habit, in hope of worldly increase. He does not know if he will last the day, yet worries about the next hundred years.

Since the dog does not expect more than he needs from the carcass of this world, he is better than the one who is constantly burning with the fire of greed. (EN 239)

[1] This refers to the Prophetic Tradition: "The world is like a carcass and the seeker after it a dog." Foruzānfar, *Aḥādith-e Mathnawi*, Tehran, 1982, pp. 215-216.

Desires are like sleeping dogs; good and evil are hidden in them. When a carcass comes into view, the blast of the trumpet of greed suddenly arouses the dogs. When a donkey becomes a carcass in the neighborhood, a hundred sleeping dogs are awakened by it.

Every hair on every dog bristles like a fang, though they wag their tails fawningly for the sake of gaining their object. In this body of ours a hundred such dogs are sleeping; when they have no prey, they are hidden. (MM V 626-634)

A dog bit a desert-dweller in the leg with poisonous ferocity. The poor man could not sleep that night because of the pain. He had a young daughter. She was hard on her father, taunting him, "After all, don't you have teeth yourself?"

After the wretched man broke down and cried, he laughed, exclaiming, "O father's little delight! Though I was more powerful than the dog, I would still be restrained about using my jaws and teeth. Even if an arrow were aimed at my head, I would still not bite a dog in the leg. One may be harsh with worthless folk, but a person should not become a dog." (B 947)

Whenever a stick beats down on a dog, his ignorance is such that he bites it. The stick is merely a medium; it has no will of its own being wielded by a hand. I am such a stick in the hand of God's Wrath, which beats the dog-tempered ones. (HAu 37)

Dogs are kind to one another, when there is no provocation in sight. Throw a morsel amongst them, though, and they will tear at each other's flanks. (Sa'di)

All are the descendants of Adam; all are human. Some are inclined towards good, some towards evil. One would not harm an ant, while another is more ignoble than a dog. (Sa'di)

One does not normally do good towards the unworthy, although occasionally one may do it for reasons of expediency.

When the savage dog sharpens his teeth, give him a bone immediately. There is nothing worse in the world than a dog; to be kind to him is not unwise. You train him for battle by throwing stones at him, and if you keep him cowed, he will look after your flock.(Sa‘di)

Wash the dog in the seven seas and the wetter he gets, the more filthy he becomes. If you take Jesus' donkey to Mecca, he is still a donkey when he gets there.(G 434)

Even if a filthy person puts on the shirt of Shebli or Ma‘ruf everyone knows that his dog-like filthiness cannot be washed away. (Sa‘di)

Even if you have become a Korah[1] in wealth; of course, a dog in a golden collar is still the same dog. (Sa'di)

If you're a human being, don't overeat, for the dog demeans himself badly by being a glutton. (G 136)

The hungry one is a slave to adversity, his back to society and his face to the wall. Better to be like the dogs of the stable, who fawningly wag their tails for a morsel. (HAu 120)

[1] The nephew of Moses famous for his wealth and avarice.

Don't fawn like a dog for the sake of some food; don't be attached to a couple of loaves hung from the saddle. (HAu 924)

Anger with others is dog-like and bestial; and this dog-like bestiality comes from lack of wisdom. How could one who is aided by wisdom succumb to being a beast? (HAu 281)

The body contains the lust of a horse and the anger of a dog; have the discipline to hold them both in moderation. (HH 374)

Cast the dog of spite out of your breast; do not bring the dog in your breast into your daily prayers (*namāz).* (HH 280)

I moan like a lion out of pain for the fox of Your love, though that fox takes me for a prattling dog. (Sa'di)

Seeking Union, while his rivals defame him behind his back, Jāmi wanders the streets, a dervish, pursued by the clamor of dogs. (Jāmi)

A dog always attacks the poor; so far as it can, it inflicts wounds on the poor. (MM III 2437)

The dog rushes angrily at dervishes; while the moon smears her eyes with the dust of the feet of dervishes. (MM II 2355)

The dog tears dervishes' garments, while the rest of the world is their slave. (HH 491)

How can one complain of an oppressor living in your reign, when you yourself support his oppression? The dog who tears the traveler's garment is not to be blamed, but the ignorant farmer who trained it. (B 278)

A prayer for the dog:

I have mercy on all the unbelievers, for souls are the bounty of God. I have pity and forgiveness for dogs, saying to myself, "Why do they suffer chastisement from the stones that are cast at them?"

I utter a prayer for the dog that bites, crying, "O God, deliver him from this evil disposition! Keep also these dogs in that good thought, so that they may not be stoned by the people." (MM III 1800-1,804)

ABBREVIATIONS

AN *Asrār-nāma*
AT *Asrār at-tauḥid*
B *Bustān*
EN *Elāhi-nāma*
G *Golestān*
HAu *Ḥaft aurang*
HH *Ḥadiqat al-ḥaqā'eq*
KAM *Kashf al asrār*
MAr *Manāqeb* (Auḥadi Kermāni)
MM *Mathnawi-ye ma'nawi*
MN *Moṣibat-nāma*
MRM *Montakhab-e Raunaq al-majāles*
MT *Manṭeq aṭ-ṭair*
NfO *Nafaḥāt al-ons*
OT *Ons at-tā'ebin*
RJn *Rauḍhāt al-jenān*

RQ *Resāla-ye Qoshairiya*
SKS *Sirat-e Shaikh Abu 'Abdo'llāh ebn Khafif*
T *Tamhidāt*
TA *Tadhkerat al-auliyā'*

BIBLIOGRAPHY

Aflāki, Shamso'd-Din Aḥmad, *Manāqeb al--'arefin.* 2 vols., Ankara, 1959-60.

'Ameli, Bahā'od-Din Mohammad. See Shaikh Bahā'i.

'Aṭṭār, Naishāburi Farido'd-Din. *Asrār-nāma.* Ed. Sayyed Ṣādeq Gauharin. Tehran, 1959.

__.*Diwān-e qasā'ed wa tarji'āt wa ghazaliyāt.* Ed. Sa'id Nafisi. Tehran, 1960

__.*Elāhi-nāma.* Ed. Helmut Ritter. Tehran, 1980.

__.*Manṭeq aṭ-ṭair* Ed.Sayyed Ṣādeq Gauharin. Tehran, 1977.

__.*Moṣibat-nāma.* Ed. Nurāni Weṣāl. Tehran, 1977.

__.*Tadhkerat al-auliyā'.* Ed. Moḥammad Este'lāmi. Tehran, 1975.

Bokhāri, Abu 'Abdo'llāh Moḥammad ebn Esmā'il. *Jāme' aṣ-ṣaḥiḥ.* Ed. L. Krehl and W. Juynball, leiden, 1862-1908, and Cairo, 1956-57.

Dailami, Abo'l-Ḥasan. *Sirat-e Shaikh-e Kabir Abu*

'Abdo'llāh ebn Khafif-e Shirāzi. Persian trans. Rokn'd-Din Yaḥyā ebn Jonaid Shirāzi. Ed. Annemarie Schimel. Preface and notes by Dr. Taufiq Sobḥāni. Tehran, 1981.

Ebn Karbalā'i, Ḥāfeẓ Ḥosain. *Rauḍhāt al-jenān wa jannāt al-janān.* Ed. Ja'far Solṭānio'l-Qorrā'i. Tehran, 1965.

Hamadāni, 'Aino'l-Qoḍhāt. *Tamhidāt.* Ed. 'Afif 'Osairān. Tehran, 1962.

Jām, Shaikh Aḥmad (Zenda Pil). *Ons at-tā'ebin wa ṣerāṭ Allāh al-mobin. Ed.* 'Ali Fāḍhel. Tehran,1971.

Jāmi, 'Abdo'r-Raḥmān. *Diwān-e kāmel-e Jāmi.* Ed. Hāshem Rāḍhi. Tehran, 1962.

__.*Haft aurang.* Ed. Mortaḍhā Gilāni. Tehran, 1978.

__.*Nafaḥāt al-ons.* Ed. Mehdi Tauḥidipur. Tehran, 1964.

Kermāni, Auḥado'd-Din. *Manāqeb.* Ed. Badi'o'z-Zamān Foruzānfar. Tehran, 1969.

Khojandi, Kamāl. *Diwān-e Kamālo'd-Din Mas'ud Khojandi.* Ed. 'Aziz Daulatābādi. Tehran, 1958.

Maibodi, Abo'l-Faḍhl Rashido'd-Din. *Kashf al-asrār wa 'oddat al-abrār.* 10 vols. Ed. 'Ali-Asghar Ḥekmat. Tehran, 1978.

Monawwar, Moḥammad ebn (al-) . *Asrār at-tauḥid fi maqāmāt ash-Shaikh Abu Sa'id.* Ed. Dhabiḥo'llāh Ṣafā'. Tehran, 1928.

Moslem, Abo'l-Ḥosain. *Ṣaḥiḥ.* Cairo, 1929.

Nicholson, R. A., trans., ed. *The Mathnawi of Jalāu'ddin Rumi,* 4th ed., 3 vols. London : Luzac, 1977.

Pickthall, Marmaduke, trans. *The Glorious Koran.* London, 1930; reprint, 1969.

Qoshairi, Abo'l-Qāsem. *Tarjama-ye resāla-ye Qoshairi.* Ed. Badi'o'z-Zamān Foruzānfar. Tehran, 1982.

Rumi, Jalālo'd-Din. *Kolliyāt-e Shams yā Diwān-e kabir.* 10 vols. Ed. Badi'o'z-Zamān Foruzānfar. Tehran,

1959.
__. *Mathnawi-ye ma'nawi.* Ed. R.A. Nicholson. Tehran, 1977.
Sa'di, Moṣleḥo'd-Din. Bustān. Ed. Nuro'd-Din Irānparast. Tehran, 1977.
__.Golestān. Ed. Khalil Khaṭib Rahbar. Tehran, 1969.
__.Kolliyāt-e Sa'di. Ed., Moḥammad 'Ali Forughi. Tehran, 1978.
Sanā'i, Abo'l-Majd Majdud. Diwān-e Sanā'i-ye Ghaznawi. Ed. Modarres Raḍhawi. Tehran, 1975.
__.Ḥadiqat al-ḥaqiqat wa shari'at aṭ-ṭariqat. Ed. Modarres Raḍhawi. Tehran, 1976.

INDEX